If I Were

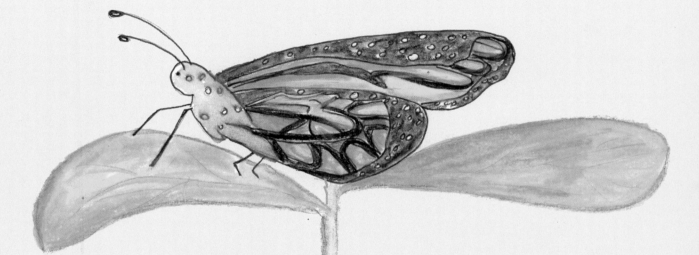

A Caterpillar

Published by: QuickTurtle Books LLC®

http://www.richardrensberry.com

ISBN: 978-1-940736-30-3

Published in the United States of America

If I were a caterpillar,

I'd inch my way complete.

While breezes come to tickle
I'd eat and eat and eat.

In my up-side-down
I'd grow fatter than a clown
munching sticky leaflets
and gulping milkweed down.

If I were a caterpillar,
I'd make my legs grow strong
and wiggle with antennae
to find my way along.

If I were a caterpillar,
I'd be icky, horned and ply
my stripes and my desire
for learning how to fly.

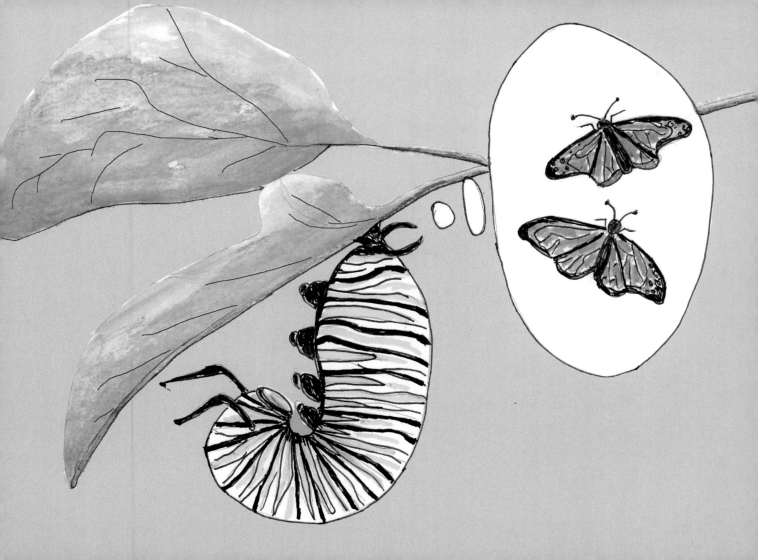

I'd strengthen my belief
in metamorphosis
and form myself a brief
home in chrysalis.

If I were a caterpillar,

I'd muster up my color
of bright orange-red;
go to sleep for days
in my soft, green bed.

If I were a caterpillar
I'd dream of deep blue sky;

I'd unfold from my cocoon
a monarch butterfly.

The End

Other QuickTurtle Books available at Amazon.

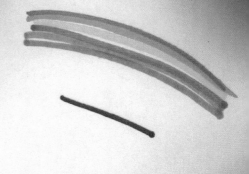

Colors
Talk

by Richard Rensberry

Illustrated by Mary Rensberry